WILD
BACKYARD
ANIMALS

Watch Out for

RATTLESNAKES!

Jesse McFadden

PowerKiDS press.

New York

Published in 2016 by The Rosen Publishing Group, Inc.
29 East 21st Street, New York, NY 10010

First Edition

Editor: Caitlin McAneney
Book Design: Katelyn Heinle/Tanya Dellaccio

Photo Credits: Cover Tom Reichner/Shutterstock.com; p. 4 Jay Ondreicka/Shutterstock.com; p. 5 Audrey Snider-Bell/Shutterstock.com; pp. 7, 9 Heiko Kiera/Shutterstock.com; p. 8 Carlos Amarillo/Shutterstock.com; p. 10 Ryan M. Bolton/Shutterstock.com; p. 11 Amee Cross/Shutterstock.com; p. 13 bierchen/Shutterstock.com; p. 15 (inset) reptiles4all/Shutterstock.com; p. 15 (main) Joe McDonald/Shutterstock.com; p. 17 John Cancalosi/National Geographic Magazines/Getty Images; p. 19 https://en.wikipedia.org/wiki/Snake_handling#/media/File:Snakehandling.png; p. 20 wenerimages/Shutterstock.com; p. 21 Guy J. Sagi/Shutterstock.com; p. 22 Steve Byland/Shutterstock.com.

Library of Congress Cataloging-in-Publication Data

Names: McFadden, Jesse.
Title: Watch out for rattlesnakes! / Jesse McFadden.
Description: New York : PowerKids Press, 2016. | Series: Wild backyard
  animals | Includes index.
Identifiers: LCCN 2015028138| ISBN 9781508142638 (pbk.) | ISBN 9781508142645
  (6 pack) | ISBN 9781508142652 (library bound)
Subjects: LCSH: Rattlesnakes–Juvenile literature.
Classification: LCC QL666.O69 M395 2016 | DDC 597.96/38–dc23
LC record available at http://lccn.loc.gov/2015028138

Manufactured in the United States of America

CPSIA Compliance Information: Batch #BW16PK: For Further Information contact Rosen Publishing, New York, New York at 1-800-237-9932

CONTENTS

WHAT'S THAT RATTLE?

Imagine you're playing in your backyard, when suddenly you hear a rattling sound. You look behind you and see a snake curled up on the ground. Watch out—it's a rattlesnake!

There are around 30 species, or kinds, of rattlesnakes living throughout North and South America. They're found in meadows, wetlands, deserts, and even backyards. It's important to know what to do if you come face to face with this fearsome snake.

EASTERN DIAMONDBACK

BACKYARD BITES
Eastern diamondback and western diamondback rattlesnakes both have a diamond pattern on their skin.

TWO COMMON RATTLESNAKES IN NORTH AMERICA ARE THE EASTERN DIAMONDBACK, PICTURED TO THE LEFT, AND THE WESTERN DIAMONDBACK, PICTURED HERE.

RATTLESNAKE RANGE

Could you find a rattlesnake in your backyard? If you live in certain areas of North and South America, it's a possibility. The possibility is higher if you live in the southwestern United States.

Western diamondbacks are found in southwestern states such as Arizona, California, New Mexico, and Texas. Eastern diamondback rattlesnakes live in the southeastern United States—from the Carolinas to Florida. They're found as far west as the Mississippi River. You might find them in the woods or near the coast.

BACKYARD BITES

The eastern diamondback rattlesnake can be found in the Florida Everglades. This is an area of shallow water with tall grasses and small islands. It's also home to the American alligator and the **rare** Florida panther!

A RATTLESNAKE'S FAVORITE HABITAT IS LAND WITH SOME GRASS, ROCKS, OR BRUSH TO HIDE IN. THIS HELPS IT HIDE FROM PREDATORS AND SNEAK UP ON PREY.

CANADA

UNITED STATES

MEXICO

ATLANTIC OCEAN

PACIFIC OCEAN

SOUTH AMERICA

RATTLESNAKE TERRITORY

FEARSOME SNAKE FEATURES

If you see a snake, it's important to be able to **identify** it. While many snakes aren't **venomous**, the rattlesnake certainly is. Rattlesnake size depends on the species. Most are around two to four feet (0.6 m to 1.2 m) long. The longest rattlesnake species, eastern diamondbacks, can grow to eight feet (2.4 m) long!

Rattlesnakes are usually brown, dark green, black, or gray. Different species have different patterns on their skin. Their skin color and patterns help them blend in with their surroundings.

BACKYARD BITES

Rattlesnakes have teeth that are long, hollow, and very sharp. They're called fangs, and they can deliver a venomous bite.

THE EASIEST WAY TO IDENTIFY A RATTLESNAKE IS BY ITS RATTLE. THE RATTLE IS MADE OUT OF HOLLOW SEGMENTS, OR PARTS, THAT CLICK TOGETHER WHEN THE SNAKE MOVES ITS TAIL.

A HUNTER'S SUPERSENSES

Rattlesnakes are great hunters because of their amazing senses. On the hunt, a rattlesnake's forked tongue will flick in and out. The tongue picks up smells and passes them over a smelling **organ** on the roof of the snake's mouth.

Rattlesnakes have a great sense of vision. They're also called pit vipers, which means they have a heat-sensing pit organ located between each eye and nostril. This helps rattlesnakes sense prey that are nearby just by their heat. With these supersenses, a rattlesnake can hunt in the dark.

BACKYARD BITES

Rattlesnakes can strike prey or an enemy at a speed of about half a second!

BACKYARD BITES
A rattlesnake can go for about two weeks without eating. It only hunts when it's hungry.

ONCE A RATTLESNAKE LOCATES ITS PREY, IT STRIKES FORWARD AND BITES THE PREY WITH ITS VENOMOUS FANGS. THEN, IT LETS GO AND FOLLOWS THE PREY BY SCENT AS IT TRIES TO ESCAPE. WHEN THE ANIMAL HAS DIED, THE RATTLESNAKE FEASTS.

A RATTLESNAKE'S DIET

With its surprise attacks, supersenses, and venom, the rattlesnake is a top predator in its **ecosystem**. It likes to eat small mammals, such as mice, rats, squirrels, and rabbits. It'll eat a bird if it can catch and hold it. Desert rattlesnakes even eat lizards.

Rattlesnakes are also prey for other animals. Big birds of prey, such as eagles and hawks, like to eat rattlesnakes. Kingsnakes also eat rattlesnakes. Rattlesnakes have to look out for coyotes, bobcats, and foxes, too.

LIKE MANY OTHER SNAKES, RATTLESNAKES DON'T CHEW THEIR FOOD—THEY SWALLOW IT WHOLE.

BACKYARD BITES

After a meal, a rattlesnake will hide out for a while. In that time, the rattlesnake **digests** its meal.

VERY VENOMOUS

Rattlesnake venom can kill small animals and cause serious harm to humans. Some bites are even deadly, or fatal. The strength of a rattlesnake's venom depends on its species. Some are more venomous than others.

Rattlesnakes can decide how much venom they want to use. Some bites are "dry bites," which means the snake bites but doesn't release venom. Young snakes are sometimes more dangerous because they can't control how much venom they let out.

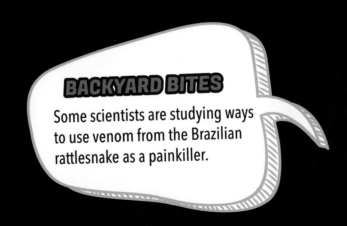

BACKYARD BITES

Some scientists are studying ways to use venom from the Brazilian rattlesnake as a painkiller.

SOME SNAKES, SUCH AS THE KINGSNAKE, AREN'T HARMED BY RATTLESNAKE VENOM. THAT MAKES THE KINGSNAKE A POWERFUL PREDATOR.

KINGSNAKE

BABY RATTLESNAKES

Rattlesnake homes are called dens. They live in between rocks and in underground **burrows**. In the springtime, female rattlesnakes give birth to fully formed babies.

Unlike many snakes that are born in eggs, rattlesnakes are wrapped in a clear wrapper. When they come out of the wrapper, they're ready for the hunt. As they grow, they shed their skin, which makes a new segment on their rattle each time. Although young rattlesnakes are independent, they might share a den with other members of their family.

BACKYARD BITES
Baby rattlesnakes have to watch out for bigger animals. Their small size makes them easy prey.

SOME RATTLESNAKES HIBERNATE, OR GO INTO A LONG, SLEEP-LIKE STATE, IN THE WINTERTIME. THEY MOVE TO DENS FOR THEIR HIBERNATION AND LEAVE IN THE SPRING.

RATTLESNAKES ATTACK!

Will rattlesnakes attack people? The good news is rattlesnakes would rather slither away quietly than bite you. They're not **aggressive** toward people, and people are a much greater risk to rattlesnakes.

A rattlesnake's venom is weaker than many other venomous snakes, including cobras. There are about 8,000 bites from venomous snakes each year in the United States. Only about five of those bites are fatal, and the number of bites from rattlesnakes is even smaller.

BACKYARD BITES

In October 2005, a 54-year-old man was fatally bitten by an eastern diamondback rattlesnake that a neighbor found in her yard.

FOR MANY YEARS, SOME PEOPLE IN APPALACHIA HAVE PRACTICED SNAKE HANDLING AS PART OF THEIR FAITH. HANDLING RATTLESNAKES CAN LEAD TO HARMFUL AND EVEN FATAL BITES.

RATTLESNAKE SAFETY TIPS

A rattlesnake's rattle is its way of telling predators, including people, to back off. If a rattlesnake feels **threatened**, it lifts its body and shakes its rattle to warn you. If you still don't leave it alone, it may strike.

To be safe, stay away from areas rattlesnakes like to use as their dens, such as woodpiles, rock piles, and high grasses. Make noise as you walk, and carry a stick to move brush before you walk through it.

MOST PEOPLE WHO ARE BITTEN BY A RATTLESNAKE TRIED TO HOLD, KILL, OR BOTHER THE RATTLESNAKE FIRST.

RATTLESNAKES
MAY BE FOUND IN THIS AREA

GIVE THEM DISTANCE
AND RESPECT

BACKYARD BITES

If a rattlesnake bites you, go to the hospital quickly. They'll give you a medicine called antivenin to stop the venom in your body.

21

RESPECTING RATTLESNAKES

Rattlesnakes hunt many small animals, which makes them an important part of their ecosystem. Unfortunately, the populations of some rattlesnake species are decreasing quickly. People have ruined their habitats by cutting down trees and building on the land. Many rattlesnakes are hit by cars. They need **protection** so they can continue to live and hunt in peace.

If you see a rattlesnake, it's normal to be scared. But remember, this snake doesn't want to hurt you. Respect the snake, and let it slither away.

GLOSSARY

aggressive: Showing a readiness to attack.

Appalachia: An area in the eastern United States along the Appalachian Mountains, covering states such as Virginia, West Virginia, and Kentucky.

brush: Plants that grow close to the ground.

burrow: A hole an animal digs in the ground for shelter.

digest: To break down food inside the body so that the body can use it.

ecosystem: All the living things in an area.

habitat: The natural home for plants, animals, and other living things.

identify: To tell what something is.

organ: A body part that does a certain task.

prey: An animal hunted by other animals for food.

protection: The act of keeping something safe from harm.

rare: Uncommon or special.

threatened: Likely to be harmed.

venomous: Able to produce a liquid poison that is forced into prey through fangs or stingers.

INDEX

WEBSITES

Due to the changing nature of Internet links, PowerKids Press has developed an online list of websites related to the subject of this book. This site is updated regularly. Please use this link to access the list: www.powerkidslinks.com/wba/rattle